Pharmaceutical Sales Revolution:

How Great Reps are Overcoming New Challenges

By
Scott Moldenhauer

Pharmaceutical Sales Revolution

Published by

Sales Success Press

ISBN: 978-0-9822419-0-5

Book Design by Whitney Campbell, wcdesign@maine.rr.com

Table of Contents

Acknowledgments

I want to thank the many pharmaceutical representatives, managers, regional directors and sales trainers who shared their insights with me. Without your help, this book would not have been possible.

Several people helped with the editing of this book: Diane Sears, Sharon Galbraith and, most importantly, Aaron Olson. Aaron helped me think clearly about how to express many of the concepts in this book.

Sarah Taylor, author of *Secrets of Successful Pharmaceutical Salespeople*, suggested I identify and interview top-performing reps. Her advice has made this book a more valuable resource.

Dozens of social psychologists and graduate professors contributed to this book via their research and ongoing study of human behavior. This includes Dr. Robert Cialdini, author of the book *Influence: Science and Practice*. Dr. Cialdini's contributions to the study of social influence have provided many people, including myself, with a framework for applying social psychology to the business world.

I have had many personal challenges and triumphs during the months it took me to put this book together: the stillbirth of a son, Nathan; the blessing of a mother who enjoys good health despite cancer; and the gift of a father who still laughs despite the challenges of Parkinson's disease. Thank you to the people who have supported me during this time of my life – David and Kathy Monteleone, Dr. David and Linda Bruce, Steve and Gina Montgomery, Aaron and Elizabeth Olson, Tim and Heather Hammons and many others. You are true friends.

Most importantly, thanks to my wife, Kristine, who has been incredibly patient with me as I spent many weekends at the computer creating this book. You are loved and appreciated more than you will ever know.

Introduction:
New Challenges, New Solutions

The pharmaceutical sales profession has changed. Gone are the days of jam-packed pipelines and open formularies. Today's marketplace offers more challenges than ever before.

As early as 2002, when more reps than ever flooded doctors offices, *The McKinsey Quarterly* published an eye-opening survey about the declining effectiveness of pharmaceutical reps. The survey uncovered the following:

- The average primary care rep visits four offices before seeing one physician.

- The average sales calls last less than 2 minutes.

- The average sales call is rapidly forgotten, as physicians are able to recall only 8 of 20 visits they receive.

Now, several years after the publication of this research, not much has changed. Reps everywhere continue to be challenged by restricted access, constrained formularies and limited face time with physicians. To complicate matters, there's no immediate solution. Management understands that the reach and frequency model has lost its appeal. Nevertheless, the search for a better alternative continues.

The sales representative is caught in the middle. Companies want more sales and they want them faster. Meanwhile, office environments, insurance formularies and industry regulations make sales more challenging.

Here's the Point:

We need to adapt.
We need to adapt NOW!

How This Book Can Help

If you're a pharmaceutical sales rep, manager, trainer or vice president, this book will help you overcome many of the sales challenges you face every day. Specifically, this book provides three benefits:

Benefit #1: Learn the insider secrets of the world's best reps. Success in the pharmaceutical industry is not an accident. There are specific patterns of behavior that cause the best reps to be successful. What are the best reps doing to create success? How can their behaviors be learned and replicated? You will learn their secrets in this book.

Benefit #2: Increase your sales, work smarter and put the fun back into your job. In this book you will see how – by making subtle changes to your approach – you can tighten your selling skills, eliminate wasted effort and develop the types of relationships that make pharmaceutical selling enjoyable.

Benefit #3: Overcome access barriers. Many industry experts argue that physician access is the No. 1 challenge facing reps today. What can you do when the doctor says he only has time for a signature? What do you say when the receptionist tells you that the doctors are busy? This book offers proven, step-by-step strategies for overcoming access barriers. After all, if you can't get to the decision-maker, what's the point?

What Makes This Book Different?

There are dozens of factors that make this book different from anything you've read about pharmaceutical sales. Three of the more important differences include the following:

Rep-Driven Solutions. The systems presented in this book were not adapted from other industries, nor were they created by "industry consultants." The systems in this book were created by award-winning reps with real-world experience. As a result, they are highly effective when applied in high-volume physician offices.

Greater Precision. This book is about the finer points of pharmaceutical sales. It's about details. It's about the small things that the best reps do day after day to create superior results. While writing this book, my goal has been to isolate the subtle factors that make the best reps successful. When you know *exactly* what other reps are doing to produce results, you can integrate their secrets and take your sales to the next level.

New Perspectives. You can have the best product on the market, but without the ability to persuade physicians, market share remains flat. For the last 50 years, psychologists have been studying the process by which one person skillfully and ethically convinces another to take action. This new science — featured in publications like *The Harvard Business Review*, *The New York Times* and *Scientific American* — is referred to as the psychology of "social influence." How can you maximize the effectiveness of your face-to-face interactions with physicians? Psychologists have answers. You will find many of them in this book.

How to Use This Book

This book has been designed so that you can easily identify a particular topic of interest and immediately learn the strategies of reps ranked "best of the best" in that particular category. It can be used on an individual basis or as part of a training class.

Part 1:
Break Away from the Pack

In the new, fast-paced world of pharmaceutical sales, grabbing a physician's attention and delivering a powerful message is what it's all about. However, because physicians are so overwhelmed with demands, product messages often become buried in the daily mental clutter. Take a moment to consider some of the factors competing for your physician's attention:

- 30+ patients per day

- A rapidly aging population with serious medical concerns

- The daily deluge of dictation, paperwork and administrative demands

- Up to 10 rep visits per day

- Managed care constraints and guidelines

- Multiple incoming and outgoing phone calls, letters and e-mails

- Etc., etc., etc.

How do you make your messages cut through the clutter? How do you make your messages impact behavior? Moreover, how do you do all of these things during the course of a two-minute sales call?

The answer? You get really, really good at creating messages that are attention-grabbing, memorable and compelling. This section shows you how to do just that.

Chapter 1

Attention, Please!

How to Capture and Keep the Interest of Busy Physicians

Do you get the feeling that the physician isn't listening? Does the physician seem distracted? If you want to change the way doctors feel about your products, you first have to capture and maintain their interest. After all, if the physician isn't paying attention to your message – if your message isn't "getting into" the physician's mind – what's the point?

In the hustle-and-bustle atmosphere of a busy medical practice, keeping the physician's attention isn't always easy. The strategies presented in this chapter will show you how to keep physicians attentive, interested and engaged.

1. Make It Rhetorical

I used to have a regional business manager who talked in questions. Instead of saying, "We need better pre-call planning," he would say, "Why do we need better pre-call planning?" Instead of saying, "Pre-call planning is the key to our success," he would say, "Why is pre-call planning the key to our success?" He wasn't really looking for answers. He just wanted us to think.

Research shows that rhetorical questions set people into a listening mode (McCronskey, 2005).

Here's the Point:

If you want physicians laser-focused on your message, ask rhetorical questions.

3

Here are three ways you can increase market share by asking rhetorical questions:

- **Draw attention to product benefits.** You definitely want physicians attentive when you're discussing the benefits of your product. To do this, place rhetorical questions between your feature and benefit statements. You say, "My product does not lower the seizure threshold." You add the rhetorical question, "Why is this important to you?" Then you say, "As a physician who treats patients with seizure disorders, when you select my product, you avoid the risk of sending your patients into seizure." After stating any product feature, ask the physician one of the following questions: "Why does this matter?" "How will this help you?" and "What does this mean to your patients?"

- **Eliminate daydreaming.** President's Club Winner Sally Hodges said, "When you're dealing with a distracted physician, sprinkle your presentation with questions." Questions provide you with a way to take physicians out of a preoccupied mode and into a listening mode. Say, "I want to run this by you. Can you give me your opinion?"

- **Present clinical studies in an engaging manner.** Rhetorical questions offer a great way to spice up clinical studies. For example, rather than saying, "Doctor, I want to talk to you about a study entitled, 'The Effects of a Dietary Portfolio of Cholesterol-Lowering Foods vs. Lovastatin,'" say, "Doctor, this study asks an important question: If you want to reduce your cholesterol, which works best – diet or statins?" Do you see how the rhetorical question does a better job of capturing interest?

2. Feed the Eyes

Do you want physicians to remember more about your presentations? Use a visual aid. One study measured message recall after three days. In each condition, the communicator (a) shared a verbal message only, (b) shared a visual message only, or (c) shared a verbal message reinforced with a visual aid.

What did the researchers find? Presenting in a verbal-only format resulted in 10% recall, and presenting in a visual-only format resulted in 20% recall. However, an amazing 65% of the message was recalled when a verbal message was supported with a visual aid (Zayas-Baya, 1977-1978). Visual aids help physician remember the benefits of your product.

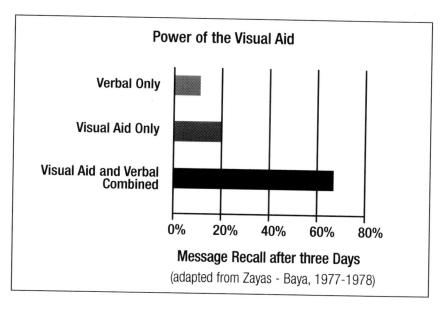

If visual aids are so effective, why don't more reps use them? Many reps simply feel uncomfortable using visual aids.

If you feel awkward about using your visual aid, consider the following:

> • **Visual aids do not determine what you say, but how much is remembered.** As District Sales Manager Gary Germek stated, "There's no rule saying that you have to flip to every page in your visual aid and give a canned presentation, but backing your verbal message with visual reinforcement can create a powerful one-two punch." *Almost any visual aid with color significantly increases recall* (Vogel et al.

1990). During a sales presentation, simply holding up a box of your samples can increase subsequent recall.

- **Many physicians prefer detail aids.** For every physician who complains about detail pieces, there are dozens of others who find them helpful. As Sales Training Director Maria Harris stated, "Shy physicians often prefer visual aids because they feel uncomfortable making constant eye contact with the rep."

- **Visual aids create a distinct competitive advantage.** One company planted "undercover" observers in the offices of busy physicians. They wanted to know how often reps use their detail pieces. What did they find? Reps use their visual aids while with their managers but rarely when they are alone (Wright, 2007). *When you consistently use a visual aid – and your competitors do not – your presentations will be more compelling.*

3. Talented Targeting

Have you ever had a salesperson bore you with talk about a product you didn't need? As you started to walk away, the salesperson finally said something relevant. You thought, "I'm not interested... I'm not interested ... I'm not interested... Hold it... IT DOES WHAT?" Relevant messages create attention and interest. They engage the customer.

While reading this book, are you focusing on each word in every chapter? Probably not. You are attending to parts of the book that are relevant to *your* situation. Physicians do the same thing. According to Regional Sales Director Sherman Phillips, "Physicians listen for what's relevant, filter out the rest, and judge you on the basis of whether you provided value."

When you target your messages – when you tailor your information to the needs and interests of the physician – you can have a profound effect on your results. Top reps report targeting their messages in the following ways:

Targeting Essentials

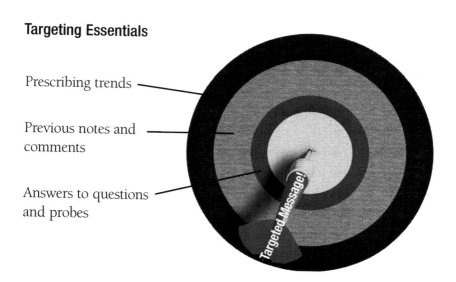

Prescribing trends

Previous notes and comments

Answers to questions and probes

Targeted Message!

• **Review the prescriber's history.** Where is your physician on the call continuum? Which issues have captured the physician's attention in the past? Do you have data to review? Tailor your messages by putting yourself into the mindset of the physician.

• **Ask intelligent questions.** Make a habit of asking physicians for their opinions. Executive Sales Representative Adam Kramer said, "Before beginning a presentation, I ask physicians, 'Do you mind if I get your thoughts on a few things?'" This not only helps you target your message, but it also helps you get more time with physicians. Doctors are more interested in the conversation when *they* are doing the talking.

• **Identify the personality type.** Which personality type is your physician? Analytical types tend to be more influenced with hard data; social types are more influenced by relationships. Keep personality types in mind, but realize that no physician is 100% in any category. *Relationships may be the driving force for some physicians, but you still need to provide the backup of clinical studies and ongoing product discussion.*

The Power of Relevance

People are more likely to act on a message – i.e. they're more likely to change their prescribing behavior – when the message is personally relevant to their situation (Sivecek and Crano, 1982). *One study found people who were exposed to a message specifically relevant to their concerns were 74% more likely to behave differently after the message was presented. This compared with only 21% of people who received a semi-relevant message* (Leippe and Elkin, 1987). As District Sales Manager Ted Sheridan said, "Successful reps tailor their messages to fit the specific concerns of each physician." For more information on how to create powerful sales messages, go to www.negotiate.greatpharmareps.com and check out the **Negotiation System™**.

Chapter 2

Power Up Your Messages:
How to Make Your Product Stand Out in the Dense Sea of Competition

There's a story about a blind man sitting on the steps of a courthouse building. He had a hat by his feet and a sign that read "I am blind, please help."

A salesman was walking by and stopped to observe. He saw the blind man had only a few coins in his hat. He dropped in more coins and, without asking for permission, rewrote the sign. He returned the sign to the blind man and left.

That afternoon the salesman returned to the blind man and noticed his hat was filled with bills. The blind man recognized the salesman's footsteps and asked, "What did you write on my sign?" what he had written.

The salesman thought for a moment and responded, "Nothing that was not true. I just wrote the message a little differently." He smiled and went on his way.

The new sign read, "Today is Spring and I Cannot See It."

This story, of course, illustrates what can happen when you take time to craft your messages. For our purposes, it expresses the following:

Better Messages = Better Sales

Over the next few pages, we examine how you can maximize your results by making simple changes to the way you communicate your messages to physicians.

1. 7/38/55

The messages you convey become more powerful depending on the nonverbal cues surrounding them. When you are in front of a physician, your facial expressions, vocal style and body movements determine whether you will be convincing.

Almost 40 years ago, psychologist Dr. Albert Mehrabian studied the overwhelming influence of nonverbal messages. He made the following conclusions:

- 7% of communication is powered by words.
- 38% of communication is powered by vocal speed and tone.
- 55% of communication is powered by body language.

This study makes an important point: *If you can master your nonverbal expressions, you can have a profound impact on your results.* Here are a few ways to take advantage of the 7/38/55 rule:

- **Leverage nonverbal power.** Sometimes it's the little things that count. Studies show that people who talk quickly are more convincing than those who talk slowly (Miller et al., 1976); people who wear dark clothes are perceived as more competent than people who wear light clothes (Molloy, 1975); and people who use happy facial expressions are more convincing than those who look overly serious (Leathers, 1997; Gueguen & De Gail, 2003). Your messages become more powerful when you master the nonverbal signals you send.

- **Share your enthusiasm.** In the middle of a fast-paced sales call, it's hard to control your voice, change you facial expressions and perfect your posture. There's one factor, however, that brings it all together – enthusiasm. Roger Ailes, former speech coach to President Ronald Reagan, said, "If you know what you are saying and why you are saying it, and you care about what you are saying, you will say it well."

- **Match nonverbal behavior.** Evidence suggests you can become a more powerful communicator by "matching and mirroring" the body language of your customers (Van Swol, 2003). For example, if you're a fast talker and the doctor is a slow talker, you may want to slow it down to more closely match the physician's rate of speech. In one study, subjects who were mirrored reported their interactions to be smoother and more pleasant (Chartrand and Bargh, 1999). This strategy may be particularly helpful when your personal style of expression is at odds with that of the physician. Representative Andy Nelson said, "I have an aggressive personality. I've noticed, especially when I'm with a shy physician, when I slow down and take a more relaxed style, the physician is more receptive."

2. Leverage Peer Influence

While doctors might want you to think they use certain products because they have conducted an exhaustive review of the literature, the reality is they often watch to see what other physicians are doing and follow suit.

Early in my career as a rep, I spent months trying to convince one of my top physicians that my product was more effective than his current choice. It never worked. He attended one of my speaker programs and subsequently started switching patients to my product. I asked, "Why did you make the switch?" He said, "Everybody at the meeting seems to think you have a better choice, so I'm going with your drug." That's the power of peer influence.

Here's the Point:

Showing your physicians that other physicians find merit in your product can have a massive impact on your results.

Here are a few ways other reps are using the power of peer influence to power up their messages:

- **Advertise your product's popularity.** Is your drug the favorite choice in its class? Make it known. Is it No. 1 in your territory? Tell people. Is it No. 1 with specialists? Share that fact. President's Club winner Gary Starr calls this the "snowball effect." He said, "When doctors discover that other doctors are using your product first line, they're more likely to do the same." Start your presentation by saying, "Dr. Martin, my product is the No. 1 choice of rheumatologists in the United States. Here why ... "

•Find cheerleaders. Take advantage of any physician's willingness to share his or her belief in your product. One rep said, "When I have a lunch with multiple prescribers, and one of them is a crusader for my product, I ask the physician to share his reasons for liking my drug. I see the other doctors, and especially PAs and NPs, perk up. It's more convincing than any evidence I can offer."

• Know how to respond to, "How's it going with your drug?" When you hear this question, realize that physicians are trying to determine whether other physicians find merit in your product. When answering, avoid saying, "Not so good. I could really use your help." Instead, reflect on where your drug is being used and share it: "This product has really become popular with physicians who are treating acute otitis media. Can I share a few examples of why so many physicians think it's the best choice?"

The Power of Popularity

Have you noticed how successful companies are obsessed with telling us about the popularity of their products? They tell us their products are the "best selling," the "top choice" and the "#1 brand." Why do they say this? They know a secret: *The more popular people believe your product to be, the more likely they are to select it* (Cialdini, 1998).
For more information on how the power of popularity can help you become persuasive, check out the **Negotiation System**™ at www.negotiate.greatpharmareps.com.

3. Repetition, Repetition, Repetition

If you want to make your messages more powerful, repeat them. Messages gain power when they are repeated (Zanjoc, 1968; Bjornstein, 1989). In fact, *physicians will rarely respond to a new product message on the first try. It usually takes multiple repetitions.*

Here's the Point:

The same message that has no impact on try #1 can move people to action on try #5.

The best persuaders build repetition into their plan. Advertisers, for example, never run just one ad. They know it takes multiple tries before people begin to "bite." In the same way, you should never give up too early on any given message.

By understanding the power of repetition, you can outperform your competitors. There are two situations in which repetition is particularly important:

• **New product launches.** If you're introducing a new product, don't be discouraged by initial disinterest. *In the beginning, it's natural for physicians to be apathetic, skeptical or even critical. When you let the power of repetition work its magic, physicians who seemed the most skeptical in the beginning can become your best prescribers in the end.*

• **New physician targets.** Executive Sales Professional Eric Kemmer shared the following story: "I used to work for a company that had an open target list. Essentially, they said, 'Here are 500 physicians. We don't care if you see one physician or all 500 – just make your numbers.' I noticed that my peers were giving up too early. They said, 'I called on him three times with no results. I'm moving on to the next doctor.' I made an agreement with myself: Call on each physician at least eight times before giving up. Because I understood the power of repetition, I quickly established a core group of prescribing physicians, minimized my workload and created superior results."

How Many Repetitions Does it Take?

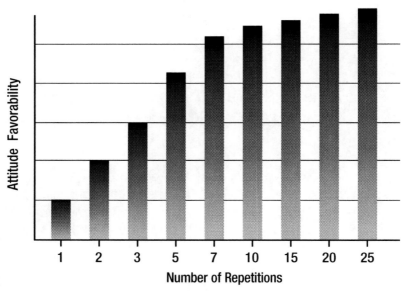

Physicians seldom respond on the first try. It usually takes multiple repetitions (adapted from Eagly and Chaiken, 1993).

Strategy #4: Talk Losses

Physicians are interested in new products and technological advances, but they often perceive them as expensive and rarely covered by formularies. "It's up to the rep to convey the benefits of his product in a compelling and persuasive manner," said Regional Director Scott Ritchie. "Physicians will prescribe branded products," Ritchie said, "if reps can convince them that their products are worth the effort."

But how can you achieve this goal when the physician perceives the generic to be a reasonable substitute? One way is by emphasizing what patients stand to lose.

Here's the Point:
If you tell physicians what they're going to gain by using your product, you will make some sales. If you tell physicians what they're going to *lose* by not using your product, you will make even more sales.

Psychologists Amos Tversky and Daniel Kahneman, who both won the Nobel Prize for their work on decision-making behavior, found that people are more motivated by a potential loss than a potential gain (1986). *By talking losses, you effectively disrupt comfort zones and provide physicians with the motivation to act.*

- If your product reduces the risk of stroke by 20%, you're better off telling physicians that patients are 20% *more likely* to have a stroke without your product.

- If you sell an oncology regimen that adds four months to the lives of patients, you're better off telling physicians that patients will *lose* four months of life *without* your product (notice that you're emphasizing losses as opposed to gains).

Sales Vice President Tom Simmons said, "Reps often phrase their messages in terms of 'happy language.' They say, 'Doctor, my product will give your patients a better 'quality of life.'" He continued, "The better approach is to emphasize consequences. What does the patient stand to lose when the doctor selects an inferior drug?"

Part 2:

The Things They Don't Teach You in Sales School

(That Can Make Your Job *MUCH* Easier!)

When you look closely at the behaviors of the best reps, you realize success is not an accident. You realize the best reps have a deeper understanding of the factors that drive results: the ability to focus on activities that matter, the ability to understand exactly what influences prescribing behavior, and the ability to quickly develop and leverage relationships.

The finer points of these topics are rarely discussed during training classes. Relationships are important, for example, but what exactly enables one rep to create a relationship in a matter of weeks while it takes another rep months or years? Time management is important, but what, specifically, are the best reps doing to eliminate extraneous activities so they can get on with the important business of presenting information to doctors? This section of the book provides details.

Chapter 3

Smarter, Not Harder: How to See More Doctors
(Faster and Easier)

Your company wants you to see eight doctors every day. It's almost noon on Wednesday, and you have only seen one. Yesterday, you only saw six doctors. The day before, you only saw five. In addition, you still have to set up two programs, respond to several e-mails and complete your expense report. How can you keep up?

In this chapter, you learn how great reps are learning to "work smarter." Rather than working more hours, they are finding ways to eliminate extraneous activities and focus on what really matters. In the end, these reps are more effective, more relaxed and more satisfied with their jobs.

1. Work Smarter . . . Call Before You Drive

When asked about her strategies for working smarter, Specialty Representative Arlene Jennings said, "Maximize doctor time. Minimize windshield time." Another rep commented, "One of the easiest ways to pack more hours into your week is to take a slice out of your driving time."

Before making a substantial drive, call the office. Metabolism Sales Specialist Mike Morin said, "I have a 15-minute rule: If the office is more than 15 minutes away, I call to make sure the physician is in."

> "It's not the daily increase but daily decrease.
> Hack away at the unessential."
>
> Bruce Lee, Martial Artist

Make sure you have the phone numbers of your most important offices programmed into your phone. Call the office and say, "Hi, this is Sheila Smith, I'm one of the reps calling on your office. I just wanted to make sure you're in this afternoon." Offices understand that you're coming in to see the doctor. They will notify you if the physician is gone.

If you're worried the receptionist will discourage you – thinking you're going to take too much of the doctor's time – simply say, "I might be in the area today. I'm just wondering if the doctor is in the office in case I need a signature." This will put the receptionist at ease, even if you'd also like to grab a moment with the physician.

On the other hand, if you have a relationship with the receptionist, she will say, "Sheila, the doctor had to go to the hospital, but he will be back by 2:30. Try then."

Here's the Point:

This simple strategy can save you hours every week.

When the physician is out, and you call before you drive, you save yourself the time of (a) driving to the office, (b) finding a parking spot, and (c) waiting in line at the reception desk. Start calling ahead today and see how many hours you save this week.

Route it Out

"The best reps create daily maps," said Oncology Manager Paul Wedeberg. When you start the day with a routing plan – and a plan for each call – you accomplish more. District manager Robin Vaughn put it this way: "Routing achieves three purposes: (1) it gives you a logical order to follow, (2) it helps you stay on track and (3) it plants a subconscious goal into your mind that you need to see a certain number of doctors today."

2. Work Smarter . . . *Leverage Multi-Physician Offices*

Do you want to see more physicians – faster and easier? Here's a tip from top reps: Maximize the number of calls you make in multi-physician offices. Award-winning Representative Hector Juarez said, "It's easy to walk into a clinic of three physicians, get excited about seeing one doctor and walk out the door. What about the other two physicians?"

After you see the first physician–and while your confidence is up – use your relationships with nurses to get time with the other physicians. District Manager Tom Tindal said, "When you have solid relationships with nurses, they will go out of their way to help you see the other doctors."

The bottom line: *When you are good at leveraging multi-physician offices, you can accomplish more in one hour than many reps accomplish all day.*

3. Work Smarter . . . *Seize the Moment*

Dozens of surveys show the average pharmaceutical rep spends only a few minutes each day with physicians. Therefore, it's important to make each minute count.

Several representatives provided the following suggestions on how to capture more selling time:

• **Round 'em up.** Doing a lunch? When you enter the office, ask the receptionist, "Are all of the physicians in today?" You will probably hear exceptions like, "Dr. Smith has to leave by 12:30," or, "Dr. Kramer is running behind." Now you're prepared. At the beginning of the lunch, find someone who knows you and say, "Can you ask Dr. Smith if I can catch her for a minute before she leaves?" or, "I know Dr. Kramer is running behind – can you tell her I will be extremely brief?" If you're politely aggressive, the staff will get the physicians to spend time with you. Take a proactive approach on every lunch. *The extra calls will add up.*

• **Skip the small talk.** Representative Sharon Miller said, "When time is of the essence, forget the small talk and share a message. Doctors know you're there to do a job, so you shouldn't feel like you have to 'establish rapport' on every call." Say, "It's nice to see you. Can I share a quick message?"

• **Seize more moments.** Quality time with physicians often occurs over lunch, but sometimes offices are booked for months. Keep a short list of your most important offices. Call regularly and say, "Have you had any lunch cancellations?" If you get to know the person who schedules the lunches, you will receive priority.

4. Work Smarter . . . *Be an Early Bird*

It pays to be an early bird. Most reps find they can see more physicians and have better-quality calls earlier in the day. According to one survey, physicians are most likely to see sales reps before 10a.m. Later in the day, unexpected patient delays and emergencies add up.

District Manager Stephen Robbins said, "I ask my reps to save paperwork, phone calls and e-mails for later in the day. It's best to use the first part of the day for the most important aspect of your job – seeing physicians."

5. Work Smarter . . . *Quit Catering*

Are you tired of being a caterer? Sick of food being spilled onto the back seat of your car? Have your lunches delivered. Senior Professional Representative Michelle Riggins said, *"When you add up all of the hours you spend driving to restaurants, finding parking spots and waiting in line to pick up food, you realize that this is time that can be used to see more physicians."*

What if the office wants food from a restaurant that doesn't deliver? Have a list of three delivery-friendly restaurants handy. Call the office and say the following:

"Hi, this is Brian from ABC Pharmaceuticals. I'm providing lunch tomorrow. I'm planning on ordering food from restaurant X, Y or Z [all deliver]. Which one sounds good to you?"

By presenting the options in this way, offices will almost always choose from the restaurants you prefer. You can use your extra time to squeeze in more calls.

Work Smarter
(By Asking Fellow Reps)

Are you having a hard time with an office? Problems getting a lunch? Is the receptionist blocking your access attempts? Ask other reps for help. Say, "Which staff members can get you in?" "What's the best way to get an appointment?" or "Who will help me?" As one award-winning rep mentioned, *"Why spend months trying to crack the code when the rep sitting next to you in the waiting room may be willing to share the secret?"*

6. Work Smarter . . . *Reduce Cell Minutes*

Ask yourself the following questions: Are my cell phone minutes being used for business or social purposes? Have I sat in the parking lot of an office chatting with a friend while another rep enters the building, presents to the physician and then drives off to his next office?

If you answered "yes" to these questions, make sure you're keeping your phone minutes in check. As one rep said, "Everybody needs the support of a teammate from time to time, but sometimes it's easy to start a call with a business purpose and trail off into 30 minutes of social talk."

Here's the Point:

Minimize unnecessary phone time. Let social and non-urgent calls go to voicemail. Use the time normally spent on the phone to catch more physicians.

Chapter 4

How Doctors Think:
Are You Ready to Change Prescribing Habits?

Imagine you just had lunch with one of your top prescribers, Dr. Martinez. It was a great call, and Dr. Martinez committed to using your product first line. Now, fast forward to the following morning. Dr. Martinez is seeing a patient who is a perfect candidate for your product.

In his haste, Dr. Martinez reaches for his prescription pad and prescribes your competitor's product! What happened ? Was Dr. Martinez insincere when he said was going to use your product? Probably not. It's simply that your competitor's product was at the top of his mind.

What would happen if *your* product was first on Dr. Martinez's mind? What would happen if your product came to mind first for *all* of the physicians in your territory? Would it make your job easier? In this chapter, we explore four ways to change habits and make your brand No. 1.

1. Understand Top-of-Mind Influence

If you've ever heard a physician say, *"I really do think you have a better drug, but I forget to prescribe it,"* you know the power of top-of-mind factors.

More than 50 years ago, Harvard psychologist Jerome Bruner coined the term "accessibility rule." The accessibility rule states that real-world decisions are *rarely* based on careful thought and deliberation. More frequently they are based on top-of-mind factors (Bruner, 1957, 1958).

If your brand is most accessible in the physician's mind, you're in luck. If not, you have to find a way to get it top-of-mind.

Even when there is a distinct preference for a particular product, top-of-mind factors can override the rational thought process. When a physician tells you that he believes you have a better product, he is probably telling you the truth. But, in the heat of the moment, when patients are waiting, phone calls are coming in and the doctor is overwhelmed with demands, top-of-mind factors take over. His better judgment is overcome by habit.

This is not to say that physicians never think about their prescribing decisions. They do, but *brands that are easily retrieved from memory – brands that are top of mind – are significantly more likely to be selected than other brands* (Posavac, Sanbonmatsu & Fazio, 1997).

The good news is that psychologists know exactly how to make your brand top-of-mind.

Which product is top of this physician's mind? Top-of-mind products are most likely to be prescribed.

First Thought, First Choice

You may call it habit. Psychologists call it "mental accessibility." The reality is, whenever physicians need to make a fast decision about a product, top-of-mind information influences the decision that is made. During a patient exam, for example, a physician thinks, "This patient needs a beta blocker." What happens next? The physician rarely stops to contemplate the merits of each and every beta blocker on the market. Instead, the doctor makes a split-second decision and prescribes the first beta blocker that comes to mind. For more information on how doctors make prescribing decisions, go to www.negotiate.greatpharmareps.com and check out the **Negotiation System**™.

2. Hit It Again and Again

Let's look at how you can create top-of-mind opportunities. One of the best ways to get your product "top of mind" is repetition (Johnson & Watkins, 1971).

Here's the Point:

Products presented with greater frequency are brought to mind with greater ease. Products brought to mind with greater ease are prescribed with greater frequency.

Pharmaceutical companies know that the more often a physician sees a sales rep, the more likely the physician is to write the rep's product. You probably hear physicians say things like, "Why do the same reps want to see us over and over again?" The answer? Because it works.

How do you put the power of repetition on your side? Try the following:

• **Always get in another "hit."** Have you ever been hesitant to discuss your product because you feel like the physician already knows your product? Try to avoid this tendency. *Each repetition of your message brings your product to the forefront of the physician's mind, no matter how familiar the physician is with your drug.*

• **Maximize brand name repetition.** Oncology Manager Kristen Wolff said, *"You should always call your product by its brand name as opposed to 'my product,' 'our drug,' or 'it.'"* For example, imagine your product's name is Zylerg. Instead of saying, "My product is efficacious, and my product is safe," say, "Zylerg is efficacious and Zylerg is safe." Every time you repeat the brand name of your product, you create top-of-mind awareness.

3. Repeat Your Message (Without Driving the Doctor Crazy!)

Are you worried that repeating your message over and over will aggravate your physicians? As you watch television commercials, notice how some of the most respected brands in our culture have communicated the same core message, year after year, while keeping our attention and interest.

Nobody has ever burned out, for example, on Ford truck ads. This is because Ford uses what advertisers call "repetition with variation" (McCllough & Ortrum, 1974). They keep the same core message – Ford trucks are tough – but add variety. One commercial features a Ford truck weathering extreme hot and cold; another features a Ford truck navigating rugged mountain terrain; yet another shows tons of steel being dropped onto the bed of a Ford truck. It's always the same core message with a twist.

This strategy helps you repeat your core messages – without frustrating the physician.

How do you use the repetition with variation strategy with your messages? Let's assume your core message is safety. One of your messages may focus on how your product is safer in elderly patients; a second message may emphasize how your product has low risk for interactions; yet another message provides a physician testimonial that your product is the "safest choice on the market." All of the messages provide variety while reinforcing your core message of safety.

Ultimately, repetition with variation helps you keep your product benefits fresh in the physician's mind, without creating burnout.

4. Time It Right

Imagine you just had lunch with a physician. Immediately after the lunch, the physician encounters a patient who needs your class of drug. Because your brand is at the top of the physician's mind, the patient receives a prescription for your product.

Now imagine there's a three-day delay between your lunch and the patient's visit. Your product has started to fade in the physician's memory. Pre-established habits and more recent presentations by competitors can interfere. You're less likely to get the prescription.

Here's the Point:

Ideally, you want to schedule your sales calls just prior to when the physician has an opportunity to prescribe the *most* of your product.

The trick is to time when you are going to see the physician. Here are a few tips:

• **See your most important physicians early in the week.** Sales calls on Monday and Tuesday will bring your product top of mind and have greater impact on weekly prescribing behavior. Award-winning Manager Stacie Krueger said, "A good call on Friday will probably be forgotten by Monday." Alternatively, a good call on Monday should influence prescriptions until Wednesday.

29

• **See your most important physicians early in the day.** When you see your top physicians early, your brand is effectively primed in the physician's mind. This is important because your product will become mentally prominent while the physician sees patients all day long.

• **Be strategic about the timing of your calls.** If your product is dependent upon new-patients starts, and you know Dr. Johnson sees all of his new patients on Tuesdays, try to schedule breakfasts or sales calls for Tuesday mornings. President's Club winner Bill Nelson said, "I sell a muscle relaxant for back spasms. Because one of my top docs gives injections for back pain on Wednesdays, it's when he is most likely to write my category of drug. Of course, his office is my first stop on Wednesday mornings." When you're strategic about the timing of your calls, you can keep your product top of mind when it counts the most.

TV and Timely Presentations

Television advertisers continually practice the art of timely presentations. Beer advertisers, for example, run more commercials before NFL games. At lunchtime, you will notice more food advertisements. Television advertisers are trying to bring their product to the top of your mind just before you make a decision. Chicken might "sound good" if you've just noticed an advertisement for chicken. In a similar way, if you know a physician is going to have a particularly busy day – or see patients who might benefit from your product during a particular time of the week – make sure you schedule your sales calls accordingly.

Chapter 5

Turbo Charge Your Relationships:

Be the Rep Everybody Loves to Love

Early in my career as a pharmaceutical rep, I heard managers from my company saying things like, "It's all about relationships," "Relationships sell," and "Nothing happens until you have a relationship."

I started asking managers, "What's the best way to develop relationships?" They told me things like, "It just takes time," or "You have to build credibility," or "Get to know your docs on a personal basis."

Good advice. But what if you're impatient? What if you want your relationships to develop with rapid speed? After all, *in the new world of pharmaceutical selling, it's no longer about whether you can build relationships but how quickly.*

In this chapter, you hear from reps who have a special talent for developing relationships. As you begin to add theirs secrets to your own, you will find your relationships developing faster than ever before.

1. Quickly Establish Similarities

Are you meeting a physician for the first time? Are you having challenges connecting with an office member? Reps who have the ability to quickly bond with others have a natural tendency to find commonalities.

> Some of the most charismatic reps are masters at quickly finding similarities between themselves and others.

Almost any similarity has the potential to ignite a spark. Oncology Specialist Courtney Richards had a hard time connecting with a physician. She said, "No matter what I did, the physician seemed to have a general disinterest in what I had to say." After asking the staff for background on the physician, she discovered a similarity – both were married to men from Germany.

During her next lunch, Courtney brought up the similarity. "It sparked a great conversation and the beginning of a strong relationship," she said. "It's amazing how one little thing has helped us bond."

> When you uncover things you genuinely have in common with physicians and office staff – hobbies, background, beliefs – you will find yourself drawn to them. In turn, they will be drawn to you. Similarities create relationships.

President's Club winner Denise Scott talked about how she discovered the power of similarities. She said, "I used to have a receptionist in my territory who was mean to reps. I discovered, by chance, that we both attend the same church." She continued, "When I made her aware of our mutual connection, she immediately warmed up. She was polite. She was friendly. She even helped me access the physicians."

2. Deliver Value

Relationships develop when one human being provides value to the life of another. According to industry consultant Eric Bolesh, "Doctors no longer look to reps as a source of trustworthy medical information, so any rep that can rekindle that kind of relationship will be miles ahead of his competitors."

How do you provide value and thereby strengthen your relationships? Here are a few suggestions from top reps and their managers:

> • **Can the canned pitch.** According to District Sales Manager Sara Pausha, canned pitches like, "Doctor, can I count on you to write my product for your next 10 patients?" create a wedge between physicians and reps. Former Area Manager and current Account Manager Will Hancock stated, "When reps are able to discuss issues in a fluid and interactive manner, physicians walk away with a positive feeling that the rep added to their knowledge base. That should be the goal."

• **Know more.** Have you ever had a truly rewarding conversation with someone who could match, even complement, your knowledge on a topic of interest? Such conversations create bonds. Regional Sales Manager Brian Hawkins stated, "Great reps can talk clinical benefits. They read more journals, attend more speaker programs and learn from more thought leaders."

3. Become Popular

Have you been at a party when a stranger walks into the room and a friend says to you, "Oh, there's Pete... he's such a great guy"? What's your new impression of Pete? You probably feel Pete *is* a great guy — even though you've never met him.

In a similar way, when you walk into an office and the receptionist says, "Oh, there's Michelle, she's our favorite rep," others feel the same.

Here's the Point:

People follow the lead of others. If the receptionists like you, the nurses will like you. If the nurses like you, the doctor will like you. Popularity is contagious.

Becoming appreciated by the total office pays off in countless ways. You're treated with respect; you're given priority for lunches and appointments; you're provided superior access. In the meantime, you create enduring relationships.

Here are a few ways to put the power of popularity on your side:

• **Jot it down.** Knowing names is important, but knowing something about the lives of everyone in the office can make a huge difference. Senior Sales Professional Jared Zirkle said, "I get detailed. If the receptionist tells me her daughter started playing basketball and made two baskets, I write it down. On the next call, I say, 'Last time you told me your daughter made two baskets. Has she made her third?"

• **Send a signal.** Area Business Manager Janice Henderson said, "Doctors take signals from staff members. When a doctor sees that everyone on his staff thinks you're great, there's only one conclusion the doctor can make: You must be a pleasure to deal with." Now, the physician is open to a relationship with you.

• **Everyone counts.** Treating everyone in the office with respect is not only the right thing to do, it's also a smart business decision. I asked one manager why her top-performing rep won President's Club several times. The manager said, "She is nice to everyone. She treats the receptionists with as much respect as the physicians. You should see it. They *want* to help her."

Popularity is contagious. If the staff likes you, the doctor will like you.

4. Feel Free to Compliment

Think about the last time someone gave you a really nice compliment. Are you thinking about it? Now, think about the person who complimented you. How do you feel about that person? You probably recall positive thoughts and feelings.

Compliments are wonderful things.
Not only do they help people feel good about themselves,
but they also help speed the rate at which
relationships develop.

While shopping in Mexico one day, a vendor called out to me, "Hey Hollywood movie star, come look at my stuff." If you have ever met me, you know I look nothing like a Hollywood movie star. Nevertheless, the compliment made me like the vendor and I purchased his products. This reminded me of one study I read during graduate school that showed compliments help people bond, even when the compliment is perceived to be inaccurate (Drachman, deCarufel, & Insko, 1978).

The point, of course, is not to provide insincere compliments, but to realize that sincere compliments are incredibly powerful tools for building relationships. *Is the receptionist wearing an attractive bracelet? Let her know. Do you like the nurse's new hairstyle? Tell her. Do you find that the physician is more articulate than most? Make it a compliment.*

When you get into the habit of complimenting people,
you will be surprised at how they gravitate toward you.
In the process, you develop stronger relationships.

Hang in There

While top reps are good at developing relationships, that's not always easy! Remember it normally takes several encounters before people "warm up" to each other (Eagly and Chaiken, 1993). As one rep said, "The receptionist you perceived to be obnoxious on call number one can become your best ally by call number ten. It all depends on whether you're willing to ride it out."

Part 3:
When Access is an Issue

If you don't have access issues, congratulations. Skip this section of the book. If you do have access issues, welcome to the new world of pharmaceutical selling.

Industry experts argue that physician access is one of the No. 1 challenges facing pharmaceutical reps today. Nevertheless, some reps are amazingly talented at accessing even the most challenging doctors. How do they do it? What are their secrets? Is it magic? Nope. Just hard work and the application of some core principles. You'll learn all about them in this section of the book.

Chapter 6

Access Essentials
(Part I)

Killer Access:
5 Secrets of the Access Masters

How do the best reps gain access to physicians in no-see offices? How do they get beyond challenging gatekeepers? How do they get signature-only doctors to stop and listen?

District Sales Manager Vanessa Pagnotta said, "With access, it's the little things that count." This chapter discusses the "little things" – proven strategies that the best reps use day after day to gain superior access.

1. Turn Signatures into Product Discussions

What do you do when a physician approaches you in the hallway for a signature but you know he is going to zip away? Is there anything you can say to get the physician to stop and listen?

Ten years ago, it was easy to transition from a sample signature into a sales call. Today, only about half of sample signatures result in true sales calls.

The next time you're wondering what you can say to get the doctor to stop and listen, try the following:

> • **Get them talking.** Have you ever noticed how physicians are more willing to stick around when they are doing the talking? When getting a signature, try asking the physician an open-ended question. In a recent survey by Health Strategies Group, researchers found

that open-ended questions can turn one-minute calls into three-minute calls (Rosenthal & Roecker, 2008).

Now's your chance.

Do you have a *system* for turning sample signatures into product discussions?

• **Express brevity.** *Are you frustrated by doctors who "only have time for a signature"?* In 1973, two Stanford psychologists demonstrated how to get busy working professionals to take time to help (Darley and Batson, 1973). You can trigger a physician's willingness to listen, their research suggests, if you start with an *expression of brevity.* When getting a signature, one rep says, *"Doctor, I have two quick bullet points. May I share them?"* If the physician knows you're going to be brief, quick and to the point, you eliminate concern over time. *Try this strategy during your next 10 hallway calls. You will be amazed by how well it works.*

2. Leverage Your Relationships

The best reps achieve superior access when they leverage their relationships. Jeff Sanders is a district sales manager in Las Vegas, NV. He said, "The purpose of building relationships is not just to make friends, but to build business allies who can help you accomplish your goals."

Great reps leverage their relationships in the following ways:

- **Ask, ask, ask.** You probably know reps who treat the office staff like royalty but never ask for anything in return. *The best reps put their relationships to work by consistently asking for business favors.* As one award-winning rep said, "You have the right to ask to see the physicians at any time. However, when you make the staff feel special, not only do you have the right, you're more likely to be granted the privilege."

- **Know *how* to ask.** In the 1960s, psychologists found that people are more willing to comply with a large request if they first comply with a smaller request (Freedman and Frasier, 1966). In a busy, no-see office, if you walk up to a nurse and bluntly ask, "Can you help me access Dr. Jones?" the usual answer is going to be "No." However, when you (a) engage the nurse in a short conversation about your product, and (b) *then* ask for help with access, you will be more successful. It's simply a matter of knowing *how* to ask.

- **Know *who* to ask.** Some staff members are willing to help. Others are not. District Sales Manager Marty Clemmons said, "It's important to identify which staff members are willing to help. If there are three receptionists, do you know which is most likely to help? How about the nurses?" Clemmons said, "It may sound obvious, but you should selectively approach the people most willing to help."

3. Ask for an Ally

How do the best reps access physicians in no-see offices? How do they get beyond the gatekeeper? Oncology Sales Specialist Michelle Connors said, "In an office where the policy is *the doctors don't see reps,* it doesn't make sense to approach the receptionist and say, 'Hi, I'd like to see all five doctors today.'"

Here's the Point:

In no-see offices, the trick is *NOT* to ask to see a physician, but to start by asking to see an *ally.*

41

Advanced Access Skills NOW!

Recent surveys indicate that 38% of physicians can be categorized as "no-see" or "hard-to-see." More than any other time in the history of pharmaceutical sales, there is a need for reps to learn how to overcome access challenges.

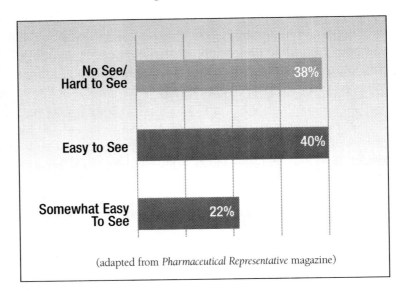

No See/
Hard to See   38%

Easy to See   40%

Somewhat Easy
To See   22%

(adapted from *Pharmaceutical Representative* magazine)

An ally is someone who knows you and likes you. Most importantly, an ally is someone who will help you. It may be a nurse or medical assistant, but office managers and even friendly lab techs can be allies.

In no-see offices, asking for an ally helps you overcome gatekeeper systems. Here's why:

• **Asking for an ally helps the gatekeeper say yes.** In true no-see offices, even if you have a great relationship with the gatekeeper, the gatekeeper's job is to keep you out. Asking for a key nurse or other ally makes it easier for the gatekeeper to say yes. You say, "Judy, is it possible to get a minute with nurse Laura? I have some information

I want to share with her." Assuming that you have taken the time to build a relationship with the receptionist, and nurse Laura, you will hear, "Let me see if I can find her."

• **Asking for an ally gets you beyond the front desk.** *Once you get time with a nurse or other key staff member, you've made it past the reception level – the most difficult layer to penetrate.* As Specialty Representative Laura Fullerton said, "Once I get time with a nurse, now I'm no longer the rep being rejected at the front desk. Now I'm 'in' with the office staff."

Overcome Access Objections

The ability to access physicians is strongly correlated with the skill of overcoming access objections like, "The doctor is busy," "Our doctors only do lunches," and "The doctors only sign for samples." For more information on how to overcome access objections, go to www.access.greatpharmareps.com and check out the **Access System**™.

---

4. Detail Nurses

In hard-to-see offices, nurses can be your pathway to superior access. *Great reps understand wonderful things happen when they start to detail nurses.* According to President's Club winner Jill Mullins, "When you take time to engage nurses in meaningful conversations about your products, you create greater potential for physician contact."

This happens for the following reasons:

• **Nurses can "validate" your reasons for wanting to see the doctor.** When your message truly has the potential to help patients, the nurse will be more willing to get you time with the doctor. After a great discussion with the nurse, ask, "Can you help me get a moment with Dr. Sanders?" You will be amazed at how often the nurse will say, "Let me see what I can do."

• **Nurses can provide a smooth transition to the doctor.** According to District Sales Manager Kim Palmer, "Nurses spend an immense amount of time with their doctors. Even the most challenging physicians can be swayed by their nurses." When you take time to know the nurse, you gain an ally who has the ability to "soften" the physician and provide a smooth transition into product discussions.

5. Help the Receptionist Help You

Most receptionists can get you in to see the doctor, but they're only willing to do it for only a handful of reps. If you want to be one of the chosen few, start your gatekeeper interactions by doing the following:

• **Start with a kind gesture.** *Do you want to trigger the receptionist's desire to help you? Start with a kind gesture.* One rep noticed that the son of a receptionist in his territory made the honor roll. He cut the student's name out of the paper and gave it to the receptionist on his next visit. "People return favors," said Specialty Representative Ron Jenkins. "When you start with a kind gesture, the receptionist is more likely to help."

• **Provide a reason.** Saying, "I'm wondering if I can get a minute with the doctor," can work. However, the request becomes more compelling when you say, "I'm wondering if I can get a minute with the doctor. I'd like to follow up on a request he had last week on how to use my new product with intravenous antibiotics." Pain Care Specialist Melissa Santiago said, "Whenever possible, I state my reason for wanting to see the doctor." One study conducted at Harvard University found people 33% more likely to comply with a request, if the request was accompanied by a *reason* (Langer and Chanowitz, 1978).

• **Override concern over time.** Why don't more receptionists let you back? It's because they fear you will take too much of the doctor's time. To put receptionists at ease, say, "Judy, if you can get me back to see Dr. Lewis, I will literally take *two minutes or less*." *Emphasize your intentions to be brief – and then keep your promise.* You'll be amazed at how often the receptionist lets you back.

Putting It All Together

No single access strategy will solve all of your access challenges. It's only when you combine these strategies that you begin to see real results. For example, when you start with a kind gesture, provide a reason, express brevity, leverage your relationships, etc., you'll begin to see amazing changes. For more information and a system that will help put all of the pieces together, visit www.access.greatpharmareps.com and check out the **Access System**™.

Chapter 7

Access Essentials
(Part II)

The Access Mindset:
Can You Really Create Superior Access
by *Thinking* Differently?

While preparing to write this book, I asked dozens of managers to identify reps they considered "off the charts" in terms of their access abilities. When I interviewed these reps, I quickly discovered they have a completely different way, both mentally and emotionally, of overcoming common access barriers.

As one rep said, "*You can have the most advanced access strategies on the planet, but unless you have the drive, ambition and courage to use them, they're worthless.*"

How do the best reps think and feel about the access process? How do their emotions and beliefs motivate them to achieve superior access? More importantly, how can you adopt their attitudes and create superior access in your own territory?

1. Access Experts are Optimists

Overall, reps who have the ability to consistently access challenging physicians are more optimistic about the access process. They believe access can be earned. They believe access challenges are part of the job. Perhaps most importantly, they believe that better access comes with increased effort.

One award-winning rep put it this way:

> "Let's face it: Half of the access battle is mental. If you have the guts to fight for access, you will become good at it. If you care enough to consistently ask to see the doctor, you *will* see more physicians."
>
> Mike Millman, President's Club Winner, Chicago, IL

Does this mean you can access every physician in your territory? Probably not. But it does mean you will be able to see more physicians than your competitors, and that's what really counts.

The effort put forth by these reps – driven by their belief that access is attainable – causes them to search for solutions. As District Sales Manager Mary Siegler said, "Beliefs about access challenges become self-fulfilling prophecies. Reps who believe there's an angle find one." Like so many other things in pharmaceutical sales, great access begins with a great attitude.

What are the two key beliefs that drive access success? They are as follows:

- **Access is part of the job.** If you truly believe access is part of your job, you will try harder and become more successful. Your mind will strive to find solutions to access challenges. Senior Sales Trainer Sylvia Brooks said, "Access is the first step in the sales process. In order to sell, you have to be able to access the physician."

- **Access comes with effort.** Access-savvy reps understand that great access comes with effort. Executive Sales Representative Josh Hernandez put it this way: "Even when the gatekeeper says the physicians see reps only at lunch, the reality is you can usually earn stand-up call rights. When you work hard to build relationships with the staff, they will help you get time with the doctors."

2. Access Experts Are Strategists

I asked managers what access-savvy reps do that other reps fail to do. Almost every manager said the best reps care enough to have a plan.

One manager made the following distinction:

"The easiest way to determine whether a rep has access skills is to watch and see what the person does before approaching the receptionist. Talented reps stop and plan their access strategy. Average reps approach the reception desk and say, 'I'm here to check samples.'"

Sam Dulin, District Manager, Tampa, FL

Reps who excel at access take time to strategize.

International sales award winner Samantha Hoffen said, "I'm constantly asking myself questions: Who can help get me in? What am I going to say to the receptionist? What is my reason for wanting to see the physician?"

The point is that access experts have a plan before they reach the reception desk. Think about your own behavior. Do you stop before you reach the receptionist to plan your access strategy? Do you think about what you're going to say to maximize your chances? Do you know which staff member is willing to help? When you start pre-planning your access strategy, you *will* see better results.

Ignore the Opinions of Defeated Reps

One manager said, "Many reps hear other reps say, 'Dr. Smith's office is a no see,' and take it for granted." If another tells you that an office is a no-see office, realize that your results, with time and effort, can be completely different. For advanced strategies on how to create relationships that increase access opportunities, go to www.access.greatpharmareps.com and check out the **Access System™**.

3. Access Experts Are Persistent

I was recently invited to speak at a regional meeting for a large primary care group. It was my second presentation on access to the same group. After my presentation, a rep approached me and said, "I tried using one of your access strategies and it didn't work." I was surprised.

I asked, "How many times did you try it?"

He said, "Once."

Realize that there is no such thing as a "guaranteed" access strategy. Rather, try to view access as a numbers game. You will not succeed every time, but the more often you try the better your results.

Don Richardson is a district sales manager in Chicago, IL. He said, "This may sound like Access 101, but the best reps simply ask to see the physician on every call." He continued, "You would be amazed at the number of people who don't even ask."

Here's the Point:

You can have all the access strategies in the world, but strategy No.1 is persistence. Ask to see the physician on every call and you will create more access opportunities.

4. Access Experts Have Courage

Think about the following comment made by an insightful rep and ask yourself whether it applies to your situation:

> "Maybe the biggest deterrent to my access is that I've just given up. In some offices, where access is tough, I've noticed I don't even try anymore. I submit my card and get my signature."

> Anonymous Rep

Gaining access for stand-up calls can be a taxing experience. You have to rely on overworked receptionists; you need to garner the "go ahead" from preoccupied nurses; you have to find an appropriate way to interrupt busy physicians. For some reps, it's too much. They quit before they start.

How do access-savvy reps differ? *The best reps find a way to keep emotional deterrents in check.* As one rep said, "Nobody likes to interrupt people, but that's what you need to do if you're going to be a successful rep. You have to find appropriate ways to get in a message, and you have to do it consistently."

During interviews, I found that all reps experience anxiety over hallway calls. The key difference is the best reps find a way to manage their anxiety to the point where it is no longer a deterrent. President's Club winner Jill Hamilton said the following: "Some reps are afraid to interrupt busy physicians for stand-up calls. They feel like they're being a pest. But it's not true. If you find an appropriate way to do it, doctors respect you for your tenacity."

If your anxiety holds you back from making more hallway calls, try the following:

• **Face your fear.** Ask yourself, *"Am I doing all I can to access this doctor?"* If not, there's probably something emotional holding you back. One rep from Tucson, AZ, talked about how she began to notice, over time, becoming timid about asking for access. She said, "I had developed such close bonds with receptionists, I felt like I was 'imposing' on our relationship if I asked them to help me." She continued, "Once I knew what was holding me back, I realized my new relationships should *enhance* my access. That was the breakthrough. Now my access is better than ever." If you're not consistently asking for access, determine why. Whatever the emotional hurdle, identify it and keep it from interfering with your ability to access physicians.

• **Give yourself a reason.** Access experts give *themselves* a reason for wanting to see the physician. Maybe they need to follow up on a program. Maybe their product has a new indication. Maybe they have new patient education materials. Reps who feel they have a reason for seeing the physician approach the receptionist with more confidence and a greater sense of purpose.

Part 3:
The Essentials
(With Teeth)

According to the popular business coach Jim Rohn, "Success is neither magical nor mysterious. Success is the natural consequence of consistently applying the basic fundamentals." The same can be said of pharmaceutical sales. *Reps who apply the fundamentals, day after day, become successful.*

You may wonder why I put this section on fundamentals toward the end of the book. It's because most reps want advanced strategies first. They say, "I already know this stuff," or, "I'm beyond the basics."

If you have come this far in the book, you're obviously interested in more than a few "fancy moves." If you've come this far, it tells me you understand the power of fundamentals. In this section, we take a deeper look at the fundamental factors that can make anyone a top rep.

Chapter 8

The Essential 4
Do These Things and *You Always Win*

While preparing to write this book, I asked regional directors, managers and dozens of award-winning reps the following question: "What are the essential behaviors that will help any rep become successful?"

The industry experts I interviewed pointed to a need to revisit the fundamentals. The essential behaviors discussed in this chapter, if applied on a consistent basis, have the potential to make anyone a top rep.

1. Develop the "Smart Factor"

During my interviews with top reps and their managers, most people alluded to the "smart factor." The smart factor means the best reps are always thinking of better ways to do their job – better ways to sell, better ways to plan, better ways to make an impact.

Consider the following two reps:

Rep #1, Bob
Monday, 8:30 - 9:30 a.m.

Bob enters a busy practice with three top-prescribing physicians. The receptionist says, "The doctors are busy today." Bob says, "OK, I'll try next week." Bob turns around, walks back out to his car and records three calls. "Oh well," he thinks, "I gave it my best try."

Rep #2, Sarah
Monday, 8:30 - 9:30 a.m.

Sarah enters a busy practice with three top-prescribing physicians. The receptionist recognizes her immediately and says, "Sarah, my favorite rep!" After a brief discussion, Sarah asks to see the physicians. The receptionist says, "They're pretty busy today, Sarah." Sarah replies, "Can you do me a favor? Can you ask if they just have a minute?" The receptionist says, "For you, I'll give it a try." The receptionist returns from the back room and says, "Dr. Sanders said he will give you a minute if you're quick."

In front of Dr. Sanders, Sarah delivers a well-prepared, targeted and compelling message. She puts samples into the hand of Dr. Sanders, looks him in the eye and asks him to prescribe her product for the next appropriate patient. Dr. Sanders agrees.

Instead of leaving the office, Sarah asks Michelle, Dr. Johnson's nurse, if she can help her get a minute with Dr. Johnson. The nurse knows and likes Sarah. As a result, the nurse tells Dr. Johnson that Sarah is a "great rep" and promises to be brief. Once again, because of her superior preparation, established relationships and selling abilities, Sarah gets another commitment from the second physician.

You get the idea. Some reps are completely focused on the process of selling. Other reps are satisfied with feeling busy.

President's Club winner Maria Martinez summed it up when she said, "If you're going to spend the majority of your week doing this job, why not get good at it? In the meantime, you earn more money, create better relationships and walk away knowing you gave it 100%." Ask yourself, "Am I leveraging the smart factor?"

2. Do the Right Thing

Doing the right thing means you're honest and proactive about the safety profile of your products. It also means you follow all company policies regarding the promotion of your products. Guidelines, including the Pharmaceutical Research and Manufacturers of America (PhRMA) Guidelines, are in place to protect patients. Disobeying them can cost you your job.

Regional Sales Director Bill Herringer said, "Being a salesperson in the pharmaceutical industry is different. Our products change the body chemistry of patients." Usually the changes are positive: Bacterial infections are cured; blood pressure is reduced; tumors decrease in size. However, in a small percentage of patients, pharmaceutical products can create serious and possibly life-threatening side effects. Because of these potential consequences, you have an immense responsibility to do the right thing.

Keep in mind that PhRMA Guidelines and other regulations bring opportunities. Senior Executive Sales Representative Brian Grapelli said, "When I started in this industry, I worked for a small company. Although I had a fantastic product, I was continually frustrated because my competitors had bigger entertainment budgets. As a result, they were able to access physicians I could not." Grapelli continued, "In my opinion, PhRMA Guidelines level the playing field. It's no longer about which rep offers the best entertainment but about who has the best product and who can clearly communicate the benefits of their products to the physician." Since PhRMA, the way to differentiate yourself is no longer as an entertainer but as someone who helps drive intelligent medical decisions.

3. Work a Full Day

Early in my career as a rep, I was befriended by a seasoned rep named Paul. He was the kind of rep who made the job look easy. He won awards year after year, but he always seemed to have time for family, friends and overall life balance.

The first time I met Paul, we were standing in the hallway of a busy clinic. As we talked, I watched Paul make three calls in 15 minutes – without trying!

Paul had developed such tight relationships with physicians that they approached *him*. On this day, they stopped, one by one, to chat with Paul. He courteously greeted them and asked if he could share a few basics about his new product.

One day I asked him, "Paul, what's the best way to become successful in this industry?" "It's easy," he said, "you get up every morning and work a full day."

I waited for the rest of his explanation, but that was it – get up every morning and work a full day. He said, "Many people in this industry cut corners. They may be out of the house all day, but they are often distracted. They talk to friends on the phone. They pick something up at the store. They end their day early."

Paul continued, "If you just work a full day – if you do what you're supposed to do – you will be successful." After several years as a rep, I realized Paul's simple advice was perhaps the best I was ever given.

Here's the Point:

You can have the most advanced sales skills on the planet; you can have outstanding relationships; you can have unparalleled product knowledge. But if you're not continually in front of physicians, these skills don't matter.

4. Take Massive Responsibility

The hallmark of a successful rep is the act of taking responsibility. In pharmaceutical sales, it's tempting to blame poor performance on outside factors: "Access in my territory is horrible" "My product has poor formulary status" "My drug is too expensive." Taking responsibility means you avoid excuses and focus on the factors you can control. "The best reps," said District Sales Manager Carol Jennings, "let their competitors dwell on excuses."

It's true that not everything is under your control. But remember, your situation is similar to that of almost every other rep in your company. Other reps also have physicians who are difficult to access; other reps also have formulary challenges; other reps also have doctors who are reluctant to try their new product. Rather than making excuses, reps who come out on top find solutions.

Top-performing reps and managers make the following recommendations:

- **Digest the feedback.** Michael Rodgers, who has been a district sales manager in Raleigh, NC, for 15 years, said, "Reps who are open to suggestions are better performers." President's Club winner Laura May said, "Receiving feedback is part of being a pharmaceutical rep, but it doesn't always feel good." Your manager will tell you things you think are unfair. Your company will ask you to make changes and imply that things you're currently doing are ineffective. Do your best to take it all in and assume that most of it is valid. In the end, you become a better rep.

- **Look on the bright side.** "You're always better off being an optimist," said District Sales Manager Mindy Snyder. "Rather than saying, 'My doctors are no-see,' begin to say, 'I haven't yet figured out a way to access some of my doctors.' Rather than saying, 'I have a bad manager,' say, 'I still need to find the best way to work with my manager.'"

- **View challenges as opportunities.** "If you can come up with workable solutions, you're going to win the game," said Regional Sales Director James Lundgren. Instead of looking at hurdles such as formulary restrictions and access as bad things, look at them as opportunities. "If you develop solutions where others cannot," Lundgren said, "you win."

The Power of Performance

Do you want job security? In the ever-changing landscape of the pharmaceutical industry, no company can offer guaranteed, long-term employment. Regional Sales Director Stanley Rollins said, "Your real guarantee of job security is performance." If something unfortunate happens to your job, and you need to find another, superior performance is the best job security you can have. "Employers always desire candidates who offer a strong history of performance," Rollins said.

Chapter 9

Closing
(for Pharma Reps Only)

The closing process in pharmaceutical sales is distinctly different from other types of sales. There's no exchange of money. There's no request to "sign on the dotted line." In fact, there's no immediate way to know whether you've been effective.

Nevertheless, great pharmaceutical salespeople know how to get physicians to follow through. They also realize that no matter how interested a physician seems to be, nothing happens until a prescription is filled.

So the question is how do you create commitments that increase market share? If you add the secrets in this chapter to your closing style, you will see better results on a more consistent basis.

1. Get Comfortable

Haven't committed to getting commitments? Not comfortable with "closing the sale"? Closing is the most difficult and the most important skill of any sales professional. If you're closing on a consistent basis, you're going to win the game.

> But what if you're not closing on a *consistent* basis?
> What if you still feel awkward?

Here are some specific steps you can take to make yourself feel more comfortable:

• **Focus on a patient type.** Brad Mullens, who is a district sales manager in the Chicago marketplace, said, "When you close for a specific patient type, you gain credibility. Being specific, as opposed to asking for every patient in a particular category, makes your request more reasonable." Narrow it down. Paint a picture of the ideal patient. You will feel more comfortable making the request.

• **Make it a conversation.** Executive Territory Manager Samuel Bruner said, "During my product presentations, I make myself stop after every point and get agreement. When the physician agrees throughout the conversation, it makes closing easy and natural." After stating each of your major product advantages, get into the habit of asking, "Does this make sense to you?" "Does this match your clinical experience?" "Do you agree?" When you do this, closing will become a natural progression of the conversation.

• **Find your style.** When asked how to make closing more comfortable, Oncology Sales Manager Paul Wedeberg commented, "Many reps are under the impression that the closing process has to be scripted and forceful. It's not true. The best closers find their own personal style." One rep said, "My company offers a class on closing. We role-played so many different closes that I finally found my own style. Now I close consistently."

2. Turn Reminders into Questions

When asked the No.1 mistake reps make during sales calls, District Manager Mike Simons said, "Because reps are uncomfortable with the closing process, they get into a continual 'reminder mode.' They say, 'Doctor, I wanted to stop by today and *remind* you to use my product,' or, 'Doctor, I just wanted to give you a quick *reminder*.'" According to Simons, "The more powerful approach is to ask for a commitment."

In other words, start turning your reminders into questions. Say, "Doctor, the last time I saw you we discussed using my product for your osteoporosis patients. If you see a patient today who needs osteoporosis therapy, *will you use my product?*" At this point, *stop and wait.*

One study conducted at Northern Kentucky University showed that when you (a) rephrase your reminder statements as questions and (b) wait for a verbal confirmation, you can create an immediate 20% increase in follow-through rates (Lipsitz, 1989). Not bad for asking one question.

Put Commitment into Motion

Commitments are most powerful right after they are made. *You can make any commitment more effective by immediately providing the physician with an opportunity to follow through.* For example, one rep places a box of samples in the physician's hand and says, "Doctor, I appreciate your willingness to try my new product. Will you give this box of samples to your next appropriate patient?" For more information on closing skills, check out **The Closing System**™ at www.closing.greatpharmareps.com.

3. Master "Time-Lag" Selling

In pharmaceutical sales, there is generally a time lag between (a) the physician's *commitment* to prescribe your product and (b) the physician's *opportunity* to prescribe your product.

On Monday, for example, the physician may tell you how she plans to prescribe more of your product, but the physician may not encounter a patient needing your class of drug until Friday. In the meantime, many things can happen: Sometimes the physician forgets; sometimes old habits take hold; sometimes competitors intervene.

The best reps proactively take steps to reduce the challenges of time-lag selling, including the following:

• **Make it easy.** You can get the most sincere commitment ever, but if it's difficult for physicians to prescribe your product, it won't happen. President's Club winner Amy Hoffen said, *"The easier it is for a physician to take action, the more likely the physician will be to follow through."* Another rep from San Diego said, "Making sure the physician has the dosing committed to memory and putting your samples in a highly-visible area are small things that can make a huge difference."

• **Anticipate glitches and address them up front.** Even when physicians sincerely intend to use your product, the smallest deterrent can interfere. *The best strategy is to proactively identify potential glitches and address them up front.* Does the staff know how to handle insurance objections and prior authorizations? Does the physician understand how to coach the patient through potential side effects? Identify anything that can deter the prescription from being filled and proactively address it.

• **Reinforce the commitment.** Like anything, *commitments fade in memory. They need to be refreshed.* Great reps continue to remind physicians of previous commitments. One rep says playfully, "You know, Dr. Sanders, I'm very persistent, so when you told me that you're going to start writing my product first line, you unleashed my determined side. So I have to ask, can I still count on you to do it?"

Psychology of Closing

Closing works because all people, including physicians, are socialized to honor their commitments (Cialdini, 1998). Parents, teachers and other important people in our lives have continually stressed the importance of keeping promises. As a result, people feel an almost obsessive need to follow through on their verbal agreements. *From a selling perspective, if a physician says, "Yes, I will try your product this week," you have dramatically increased the probability it will happen.* For more information on closing skills, visit www.closing.greatpharmareps.com.

---

4. Elicit Sincerity

While discussing the closing process, President's Club winner Terri Stanovich said the following:

> "In pharmaceutical sales, there's a big difference between a real commitment and an 'I'll-agree-to-get-you-off-my-back' commitment."

Everybody can relate to a physician who agrees to use your product but never does. *The best closers are masters at eliciting sincere commitments.* They have an unusual ability to make physicians feel so comfortable that they willing to disclose their true thoughts.

How do you elicit sincerity? It may be easier than you think: Just ask for it. Representative Amanda Phillips says, "Doctor Sanchez, I want to ask you a question . . . *and please feel free to be brutally honest with your reply.*" Another rep smiles and says, "Doctor, I want to ask you one final question. Before I do, please realize . . . *there's nothing you can say to hurt my feelings.*"

Each rep closes in a way that keeps the situation light and friendly, but also in a way that gets the physician to express his or her true thoughts.

There are two benefits to this approach. First, it helps the physician make a real commitment, meaning you create true behavior change. Second, it helps you uncover silent objections.

District Sales Manager Cindy Reyelts said, "Physicians are nice people. Many of them will agree with everything you say, even if they don't really mean it." One rep known for her advanced closing abilities put it this way: "In pharmaceutical sales, what the doctor says is important. But what the doctor does *not* say is equally important."

5. Ask for It!

One rep spent several calls trying to convince her top physician to convert his patients to the newer, extended-release version of her product. "I couldn't move him," she said.

Out of frustration, she finally asked, "Doctor, why haven't you tried your patients on the newer formulation of my product?" He replied, "Because you never asked." Six months later, after she started asking, the physician became her top writer.

Here's the Point:

If you want to maximize your effectiveness, at the very least, make sure you're asking for what you want.

Conclusion
Time for Change

At a recent conference, I watched a speaker discuss the benefits of e-detailing. He said,"While e-detailing has substantial potential, it is doubtful that this new medium will ever replace sales representatives."

Disappointed with his conclusion, a shrewd marketing executive sitting next to me said,"That's too bad. I was hoping to eliminate our sales force."

In my opinion, nothing will ever replace the significance of the doctor-rep relationship. Is there any substitute for a warm smile, a friendly face and an intelligent discussion between two human beings?

Nevertheless, we are facing difficult challenges. In fact, some experts are asking, "Are reps still effective?"

Here's the Point:

Mediocrity is not an option. More than any other time
in the history of pharmaceutical sales, there is a need for reps
who can overcome new challenges and find
more effective ways to sell.

In this book, my goal has been to share the secrets of reps who continue to excel despite challenging circumstances. I hope that this book has shed some light on how they do it. More importantly, I hope that you will begin integrating their secrets into your own behavior.

In the meantime, I wish you continued success in your career as a pharmaceutical sales representative. Despite changes, it continues to be a rewarding, important and exciting career.

References

Ailes, R. (1989). *You Are the Message*. New York: Doubleday.

Bjornstein, R. F. (1989). "The Role of Affect in the Mere Exposure Effect: Evidence from Psychophysiological and Individual Differences Approaches," *Personality and Social Psychology Bulletin*, Vol. 27, No. 7, 889-898.

Bruner, J. S. (1957). "On Perceptual Readiness," *Psychological Review*, 64, 123-152.

Bruner, J. S. (1958). "Social psychology and perception." In E.E. Maccoby, T. M. Newcomb, & E. L. Hartley (Eds.), *Readings in Social Psychology* (3rd ed.). New York: Holt, Rinehart, & Winston.

Chartrand, T. L., & Bargh, J. A. (1999). "The chameleon effect: The perception-behavior link and social interaction," *Journal of Personality and Social Psychology*, 76, 893-910.

Cialdini, R. (1998). *Influence: Science and Practice*. Revised edition. New York: Harper Collins.

Drachman, D., deCarufel, A., & Insko, C. A. (1978). "The Extra Credit Effect in Interpersonal Attraction," *Journal of Experimental Social Psychology*,14, 458-467.

Eagly, A. H., and Chaiken S. (1993). *The Psychology of Attitudes*. Orlando, FL: Harcourt Brace Jovanovich College publishers.

Elling, M., Fogle, H, McKhaan, C. & Simon, C. (2002, August). "Making More of Pharma's Sales Force," *The McKinsey Quarterly*.

Freedman, J. L., & Fraser, S. C. (1966). "Compliance Without Pressure: The Foot-in-the-door Technique," *Journal of Personality and Social Psychology*, 1966, 4, 196-202.

Gueguen, N & De Gail, M. (2003). "The Effect of Smiling on Helping Behavior: Smiling and Good Samaritan Behavior," *Communication Reports*, 16(2), 133-140.

Johnson, H. H., and Watkins, T.A. (1971). "The Effects of Message Repetition on Immediate and Delayed Attitude Change," *Psychonomic Science*, 22, 101-103.

Langer, E., Blank, A., & Chanowitz, B. (1978). "The Mindlessness of Ostensibly Thoughtful Action: The Role of 'Placebic' Information in Interpersonal Interaction," *Journal of Personality and Social Psychology*, 36, 635-642.

Leathers, D. G. (1997). *Successful Nonverbal Communication* (3rd ed.). Boston, MA: Allyn & Bacon.

Leippe, M. & Elkin, R. (1987). "When Motives Clash: Issue Involvement and Response Involvement as Determinants of Persuasion," *Journal of Personality and Social Psychology*, 52, 266-278.

Lewin, K. (1947). Group decision and social change. In T. M. Newcomb & E. L. Hartley (Eds.), *Readings in Social Psychology* (pp. 330-344), New York: Holt.

Lipsitz, A., K., Kallmeyer, M. Ferguson, and A. Abas (1989). "Counting on Blood Donors: Increasing the Impact of Reminder Calls." *Journal of Applied Social Psychology*, 19-25.

McCroskey, J. (2005). *Introduction to Rhetorical Communication* (9th ed.). Allyn & Bacon.

McCullough, J. L., and Ostrom, T. M. (1974). "Repetition of Highly Similar Messages and Attitude Change," *Journal of Applied Psychology*, 59, 395-397.

Mehrabian, A. (1971). *Silent Messages*. Wadsworth, Belmont, California.

Miller, N., Maruyama, G., Beaber, R. J., & Valone, K. (1976). "Speed of Speech and Persuasion," *Journal of Personality and Social Psychology*, 34, 615-624.

Molloy, John (1975). *Dress for Success*. New York: P.H. Wyden.

Peskin, M., & Newell, F. N. (2004). "Familiarity Breeds Attraction: Effects of Exposure on Attractiveness of Typical and Distinctive Faces," *Perception*, 33, 147-157.

Posavac, Steven S., David M. Sanbonmatsu, and Russell H. Fazio (1997), "Considering the Best Choice: Effects of the Salience and Accessibility of Alternatives on Attitude-Decision Consistency," *Journal of Personality and Social Psychology*, 72 (February), 253-261.

Rhodes, G., Halberstadt, J., & Brajkovich, G. (2001). "Generalization of Mere Exposure Effects to Averaged and Composite Faces," *Social Cognition*, 19, 57-70.

Rosenthal, R. & Roecker, G. (2008, July). "Access Report 2008," *Pharmaceutical Representative*, 17-19.

Silberman, M. (1998). *Active Training: A Handbook of Techniques, Designs, Case Examples, and Tips*. Second edition. CA: Jossey-Bass/Pfeiffer.

Sivacek, J., & Crano, W. D. (1982). "Vested Interest as a Moderator of Attitude Behavior Consistency," *Journal of Personality and Social Psychology*, 43, 210-221.

Tajfel, H. (1981). *Human Groups and Social Categories*. Cambridge, UK: Cambridge University Press.

Van Swol, L. M. (2003). "The Effects of Nonverbal Mirroring on Perceived Persuasiveness, Agreement With an Imitator, and Reciprocity in a Group Discussion," *Communication Research*, 30(4), 461-480.

Vogel, D.R., Dickson, G.W. & Lehman, J.A. (1990, July 27). Persuasion and the Role of Visual Presentation Support: The UM/3M study. In M. Antonoff, Presentations that Persuade. *Personal Computing*, 14.

Wright, C. (2007, March). "Physician Access Trends and Implications," Lecture, Center for Business Intelligence Direct to Physician Sales and Marketing Summit, Philadelphia.

Zanjoc, R. B. (1968). Attitudinal Effects of Mere Exposure. *Journal of Personality and Social Psychology Monographs*, 9, (2, Part 2).

Zayas-Baya, E. P. (1977-1978). Instructional media in the total language picture. *International Journal of Instructional Media*, 5, 145-150.

Index

To Order Copies of This Book

(888) 878-3055
or
www.bookorder.greatpharmareps.com

More Sales Now!
A Unique Offer for Sales Managers, VPs and Trainers

"Powerful. This is up-to-date information on how to overcome the challenges reps face every day."

Paul Wedeberg, Sales Manager, Abraxis Oncology

Want to see the concepts in this book come to life?
Call (888) 878-3055 to inquire about the following:

Personal Appearances at Sales Meetings • Advanced-Rep Training
Online Motivation • Customized Programs • New-Hire Training

Signature Programs:

Sales Surge:
When You Must Have a Great Quarter

Zero to Sixty Product Launch:
Secrets for Shortening Time to Revenue

Up Against the Generics:
Winning When Cost is an Issue

Big Fish Access:
How to Consistently Access High-Volume Physicians

Pharmaceutical Sales Revolution:
How Great Reps are Overcoming New Challenges

If you want to learn how these programs can get your salespeople more excited about selling, call (888) 878-3055.